Healthy Habits

EAT
HEALTHY FOODS

Vicky Bureau

A Crabtree Roots Plus Book

Crabtree Publishing
crabtreebooks.com

School-to-Home Support for Caregivers and Teachers

This book helps children grow by letting them practice reading. Here are a few guiding questions to help the reader with building his or her comprehension skills. Possible answers appear here in red.

Before Reading:

• What do I think this book is about?
  - *I think this book is about eating healthy foods.*
  - *I think this book is about how I can eat things that are good for me.*

• What do I want to learn about this topic?
  - *I want to learn about keeping my body strong and healthy.*
  - *I want to learn about foods I can eat to grow and be strong.*

During Reading:

• I wonder why...
  - *I wonder why certain foods are good for me.*
  - *I wonder how I can keep myself healthy.*

• What have I learned so far?
  - *I have learned that eating smart is a healthy habit.*
  - *I have learned that healthy foods make you smarter.*

After Reading:

• What details did I learn about this topic?
  - *I have learned why it's important to eat healthy foods.*
  - *I have learned how smart foods keep me healthy.*

• Read the book again and look for the vocabulary words.
  - *I see the word **stronger** on page 10 and the word **vitamins** on page 16. The other vocabulary words are found on page 23.*

Eating smart is a healthy **habit**.

A healthy habit is something you do to stay well.

Eating smart means eating healthy.

Healthy foods are good for you.

Healthy foods help
you grow.

Healthy foods keep
you well.

Healthy foods make you **stronger**.

Healthy foods make you **smarter**.

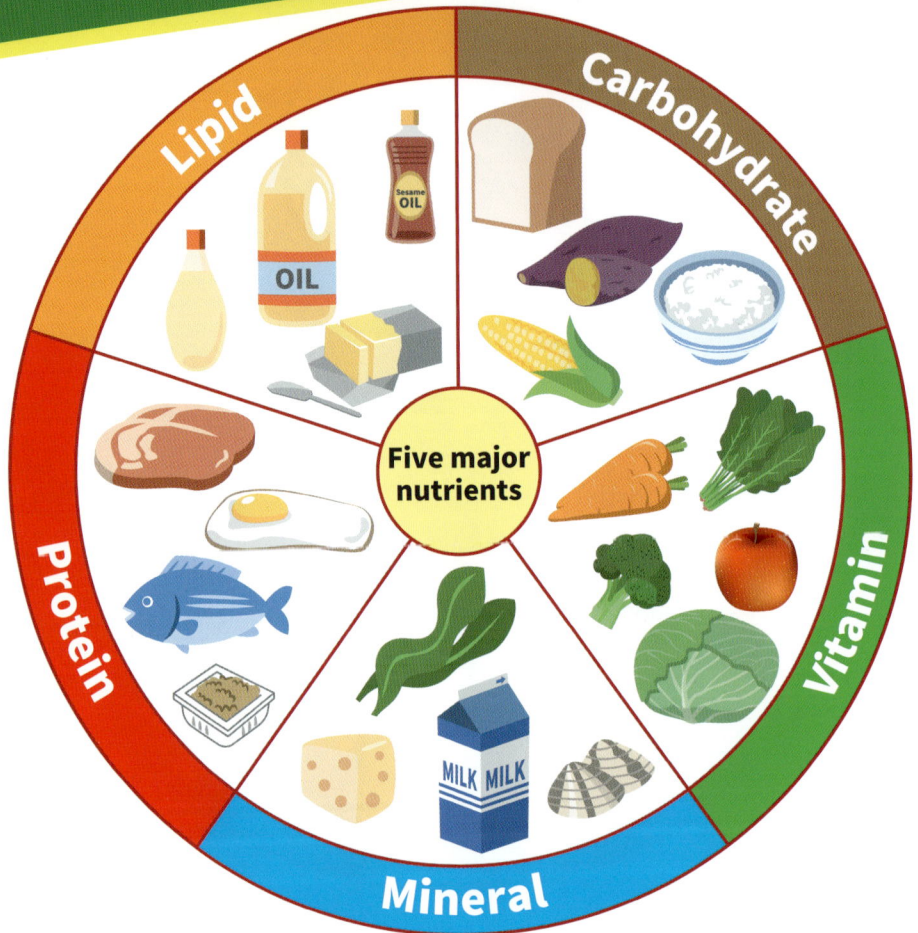

Five major nutrients

Lipid

Carbohydrate

Vitamin

Mineral

Protein

Healthy foods have **nutrients**.

You need nutrients to grow.

Healthy foods have **protein**.

You need protein
to be strong.

Vitamins

E, F A B₁
PP   B₂
K   Vitamins   B₅
D   B₆
C B₁₂ B₉

Healthy foods have **vitamins**.

You need vitamins to stay healthy.

Meat and milk have protein.

Fruits and vegetables have vitamins.

What we eat is important.

Eating smart is a healthy habit!

Word List
Sight Words

eat	healthy	milk
foods	help	need
fruits	important	smart
good	keep	something
grow	make	stay
have	meat	vegetables

Words to Know

habit

nutrients

protein

smarter

stronger

vitamins

EAT
HEALTHY FOODS

Healthy Habits

Written by: Vicky Bureau

Designed by: Kathy Walsh

Series Development: James Earley

Proofreader: Melissa Boyce

Educational Consultant: Marie Lemke M.Ed.

Photographs:

Shutterstock: Cover: Patrick Foto, Mochipet; pg 3 & 23 karelnoppe; pg 4 Tom Wang; pg 6 carballo; pg 7 Serhiy Kobyakov; pg 8 CYuganov Konstantin; pg 9 fizkes; pg 10 & 23 fizkes; pg 11 & 23 Yuliia D; pg 12 & 23 kintomo; pg 13 Roman Samborskyi; pg 14 & 23 Evan Lorne; pg 15 TimeImage Production; pg 16 & 23 Media Guru; pg 17 michaeljung; pg 18 Africa Studio; pg 19 Alexander Raths; pg 20 all_about_people; pg 21 Viktoria Bakina

Crabtree Publishing

crabtreebooks.com   800.387.7650

Copyright © 2024 Crabtree Publishing

All rights reserved. No part of this publication may be reproduced, stored in a retrieval system or be transmitted in any form or by any means, electronic, mechanical, photocopying, recording, or otherwise, without the prior written permission of Crabtree Publishing.

Printed in the U.S.A./072023/CG20230214

Published in Canada
Crabtree Publishing
616 Welland Ave
St. Catharines, Ontario
L2M 5V6

Published in the United States
Crabtree Publishing
347 Fifth Ave
Suite 1402-145
New York, NY 10016

Library and Archives Canada Cataloguing in Publication
Available at Library and Archives Canada

Library of Congress Cataloging-in-Publication Data
Available at the Library of Congress

Hardcover: 978-1-0398-0988-8
Paperback: 978-1-0398-1041-9
Ebook (pdf): 978-1-0398-1147-8
Epub: 978-1-0398-1094-5